GUYANA, MY ALTAR

poetry

by Marc Matthews

Guyana, My Altar
by Marc Matthews

© Marc Matthews 1987
All Rights Reserved

First published in Britain 1987
by Karnak House
300 Westbourne Park Road
London W11 1EH
UK

Typeset by Karnak House
Design & layout: Karnak House
Printed by Biddles Ltd., Walnut Tree
House, Woodbridge Park, Guildford
Surrey GUI 1DA

British Library Cataloguing in Publica-
tion Data:

Matthews, Marc
Guyana, My Altar.
I. Title
811 PR9275. G8M33

ISBN 0 907015 25 5

CONTENTS

First of all - is fuh me daddy of me mammie dem, an
D. opportunities dem gie me, an fuh openin' me eye
early o'clock to d-kina in justices who roam bout in va-
rious disguise, an dem faith in d-powa of d-human spirit -
Den come all dem people, some dat pass like grass an
some dat stick like sweet heart pun pants bottom -
Dem Historian dem, an dem with story dat History
writer neva know how fuh write, dem musician wha
play dem soun' backyard an record what ever happen
to Rupert Clemendored, dem Kyso man, an dem
Rhym man - is all, allyo deh hea - Kamal, Maya, J & N,
P & Z...
before you begin, tek dis in, dem ting dea fuh loud
reading. Yes.
Den cutting long story short -
Saba Saakana fuh d-neva flagging surport an encoura-
gement over dese nuft nuft years...

Marc Matthews

WHAT MARCUS TELLIN US
Edward Kamau Brathwaite

For a lang time now one know Marc Matthews

evva since the Guyanese days *a Dem Two & All a We & The Eleven O'Clock Goods a Kairi* & the LP that came outta dat creative dust

to be — since perhaps e wasn't 'publish' — the Caribbean's most important invisible verb, our leading 'underground poet' Whether at Umanayana or Queen's Park or Queen's Park Savanna/Oval, La Bassse or Vieux Fort, Bridgetown or Boston or Brixton

this brother's voice & presence & what we have to say & how he says it/had (always) to be reckoned with But where was the evidence? Where dream & strophe written down? dat precious thunder sheaf of poems . . .

The 'aura', some seh, was enough; after all, was he not, above most others, the oral poet/performer/person? The one, more than most others, who cd burn yr poems live, angular & loud & struttin or soft like olive oil & warm like fresh brown *mammie baking bread & putting me to bed* & bring dem off de page in/to yr bar/room/brawl/brain/storm or rox/y story . . .

But what Marcus tellin us

is that sound poetry is one thing pun stage/ another on the page Both must perform/yes Both will have form/yes But how trans/late trans/fer trans/form Marc calls it *oralography*: the writing of the sound: the comb the combo combination of the two: eye & ear: earth & its fire: shango & eshu: lip nto lid into lapis lazuli What in fact our so-call oral poets are coming to terms with as they extend their range from flint to flute to full & centipede steel orchestra

is tellin us

that oral/aura has its place in a tradition of attention/inattention but can be corrupted by the too-fresh laurels of applause, the audience too thirsty/greedy for the same/too same effects, the poet captured by ye claps into a riddim prison out of which he beats & beats & beats in vain/ut utter utterly like butterfly un/beat un/beat & utt/erly be/atified

what Marc moves us forward into now/then is the sight of sound: poems from our griot world of nation/nation language that can be read + read aloud: extensions & reverb into kinesis that can think, take you apart and leave you still & steady/titled skill & dreaming on yr feet how else you think this collection could so careful craft from history of Guyana: personal: autobiography of ancestors: *fuh me daddy & me mammie* dem: to the biography of places & what happened when the apple dangled down to strangle im in Eden: the silences, the exile, the razor, the cavern of invisibility/ the reasons for these things as the poems take on new dimensions: Spanish & Yoruba & QueQue & surrealism & the techniques of Aubrey Williams & the novelists and all the Caribbean here *Mountain & Morne* & Dominica & beyond that (ours & theirs/for our heirs too & ancestors) *poor/Biko/Ghandi/Shabazz/Che/Lumumba* all the victims of our blasted iconography & the bells & the cracked bells & the bells still coming in at morning at dawn with the birds where there is the beginning and no end over & over & over again

> *The T.V*
> *has my head under its*
> *arm*
> *I glap neckless on a*
> *bed*
>
> *A district of*
> *horizontal lives*
> *scream white faced from*
> *the box*
>
> *black death bands*
> *brass handles spades dirt*
> *quiet-faced priests with*
> *fertilizers in their hands*

It is not easy to write this poetry: it comes from too much hurt to mask with metaphor; it is so machete sharp it cuts before you (g)listen

But Marc sustains it, griot that he is, with detonotes of song

song always there/suffering/song always here/remembering//song building the temple/song building the wall//song swinging/song/song singing/song long

1

AN ORALOGRAPHY

When D-Dutch man
dem
fin out
Dat New Amsterdam
was Eldorado for
San' fly an' Mosquito
Dem trade it off
To the English

BIRTHTIME GEORGETOWN

Me born ah Georgetown
Hospital
Cause me did want dea
near me mudda
Demerara
Ballao & Yankee Air Base
Bauseite an'
'Boatman'
Mackinzie to Wismar
But yo see me mudda
she want dea wit
me father
So is not ups we ups
& gone

Buxton

Sy John gas light
Bright like star
fly shinin
inna Trench-Watta
Queh Queh
Kongalea
Nine night &
Wake
Conga & Cumfa
Train line
ll O'clock goods train
ll O'clock goods
Bus' yo brain
come again
Dem tie dem
Belly

Put stop
To D. govenor
An he party
mek him
know say
Life na easy
wit white
conspiracy
Ole time story
come to light
Listen to
cane
Listen to
Bamboo
Den all of a sudden
Me fadder
Tek it pun he-self
fuh go
go New Amsterdam
is not
me mudda
Me sista
an me
Wha gone pun D-Train wit he
Mahaica Michanay
ABBARY
ROSIGNAL
BERBICE RIVER

2

BERBICE

Old as plunder
Resolute as Kwayana
Beyond your Banks
lakes of Slaughter
Beds of Bones
The restless antabanta
Spirit of your
Waters
chorused by Baboons
calling
Come closer
Closer - Hear
Feed legens
whisper beneat these waters
Well we in't - in
New Amsterdam
New Amsterdam
When D-Dutch man
dem
fin out
Dat New Amsterdam
was Eldorado for
San' fly an' Mosquito
Dem Trade it off
To the English
for New York City
New Amsterdam at
The mouth of the
Berbice an' the
Head of Conje
me over canje watta
golden Gounda
song - freedom

for some
as the congregation
beat
drum
an sing
Me ova Canje
Watta
see man olay
Oh laud
stan dea
By we side
see man
Away
Oh river creek
of freedom song
flowing East to
meet the Courtanye
voyaging
to greet the Junka
in Surinama
Kalahri
Canje yr path
a   song of Freedom
A song to sing
Ova Canje watta - sing

Steady canoes
Hold tight the
Shadowing leaves
Shelter me darkness from cross haired eyes
and musket mouths
easy paddle
silent as fish fin
pull this canoe
Ova Canje watta
To meet the Juka
in Surinams
KALAHARI

3

Oh Canje
static Tounges
fill you ear
with whispering bondage
restrained
for one resounding
shout FREEDOM

an before time self
reckon wha
happen
is ova Canje
an Fyrish we
dea
each day gift wrapped
Rain or shine
a shave ice
coated with syrups of laughter
from sea wall
public road
Pasture Backdam
Duck an Drakes
on living watta
free free
To be
country in The country.

Jumbie Picnic X

4

Goodbyes invented
by Hellos
Sun ketch me
an drop me
shadow in Bartica
Gold field door mouth
A triangle of land
Where Essequibo meets
The Mazaruni
And sorrow rides
A hill white as
sand
The playing fields
Graves yard Rivers
Bartica!
watch woman
Dia Dia Protector
of Jewelled
interior
of stone ancestors
of cassava eaters
mari mari
Pi wa ri
Sultan & Tengar
Bartic clasp
of fairmaid
of sparkling-teeth
of her precious stoned
comb

5

Bartica
How many seduced
into the tangled
Mystery promise
Buried between/the rapids of
your thighs
Husband and sons
Brothers & Strangers
for each a different
face of tomarrow
Essequibo's
spoilt child
Protected once from
intruder suitors/lusting Empire Builders
By the Battle Walls
of Ky-ov-all
Bartic forbidden fruit
to the shadowed
cells of Prisoners
on the Mozaruni
Oh Bartica
metropolis of river
Essequibo
Mazaruni
Potaro
stone crusher
Mountain Mover
Tumatu mari
Scouping deeper
deeper away
the stony Barrier
Between her and
her lover
Fire.

Oh Bartica
Genis of Interior

6

FOR JAN CAREW

I K A
he clim clim
clim
lazy and weary
far behind
But I K A he
clim clim
clim
Zawa and Kabo
far behind (way dwn the line)
Higher and Higher
IKA clim
I K A climin
Wind blowing
Storm coming
Wind dying
Storm dying
Storm ova
IKA still climin
Bartica to Kaiteur
that eye
Between Land and Sky
Where Myth-ic Tears
manifest liquid Real
in a Silver-Silvered
Tear

of black Cain's Mother
The Red-skinned son
Who threw his spear
at a shadow to protect her
pierced his
prodigal brother
and she wept a
Waterfall
Where chiggaed Kai
pined and as faith
in his canoe
nailed to a sure
Current
Gave life to the
Tribe as he
Spinning and Twirling
disappeared in
Those Turbulent Sighs
veil
Tears
Day Cleanin'
night I K A not
sleepin'
I K A Climin'
Climin' a nameless
Mountain
I K A Climin'
Even when climin'
Get Weary
Climin '
I K A STILL CLIMIN'

I K A he Clim
Clim
Clim
Climin down the
Mountain

Is the Gift he
Bearin
Imagin' in
Is what holdin
Him
Climin down
The Mountain
now imagin
I K A climin
up and down a Mountain
All roads lead
To settle dwn
Georgetown
U.S. Airforce
British Army
Navy
Ol' Higue
Sucking dry
this baby
Grow more food
Posters wrapping
like commudie
Brown skin gal
stay home min baby
the seeds of anger
nourished by the
ashes of cane
Guyana Scholars
becoming Tricksters
years leap frog
into awareness
Ghana into independency
like marbles
Time hop-scotched
in fantasy
P.P.P. - P.N.C.

and the ritual
of visions seeking
reality -
Bathe in blue
eat labba
Drink Creek watta
yo mus return
The Nomads
settle down
in Georgetown
Ol' Higue
sucking you
Dry
and there was
a wake on
street of U.S.
ARMY! NAVY
Then like
a rest
An the Brown stay
Home and mind baby
And Guyana scholars
Became tricksters
Ghana gained
independency
Jummin marble
Running Bun - out
on spring top
Raiding fruit tree
to endless movie
to the last reel
spoilers

11

IN THIS AGE OF STRANGLED VISION

I walk in the razor sharp night
thinking of words that
could scream across the
wet silent surburban landscape
and burn holes into the
sleep of my brothers
wake them out of empty
compromise

SILENCE

Break the Silence
Break the Silence
Break the Silence
They demand
The Silence they
demand
With they Riot Squads
and Rubberized Gasbombs
Break the Silence
it been going on
Too long -
Break the Silence
They demand
frm Carib seas
mothers grieve
their silenced
sons

(Chorus)

Break the silence
it been going
on too long
the silence they
demand
frm spicy Grenada
to Greenham Common
break the silence
The chiming silence
Tolling the crimes
Break the silence.

Break the silence
the silence they
demand
With plastic cards
an Paperbags
of Princesses handme
dwns
Break the silence
The silence of yr
letter Box
When the Giro
Neva come
Break the silence

(Music out)
signal -
Today is yr
one an only
chance -

(Music in)
Break the silence
The silence
They demand -

POP

Tear the photo
off the wall
Rip the record
jacket clear
shade the voice
in grey curtains
open the window
clear the air
I give you
cereal flesh and
bone
A song
A voice
A beat
I am the victim
it is my black
tobacco stained voice
Dead
My wide mouth
empty now
of earth or worse

Ashes in
         the winter
               air

My slant eyes
paired sufferings
cole black hair
mild blood
I am the victim
as you of black time
black blood, black sweat
black tears

In the black hooded
eyes
of a white singer

*BLACK MAN INNA LONDON

Sun-a-hide, Rain a bus'
second time roun' inna
Babylon
an O God Winter a come
BLCKMAN Stuck a Lon
don twn.

But so help me Christ
ah not time fuh cry
NO
time fuh raise yo voice up
up HIGH
Blast each piece of stink
in' stone and
gather strength frm
Ancient voices of home
feel the sunlight deep
inna yuh bone
hear the pointa broom
scraping inna the yard
a market voice with
blessings of the land
demands in indian falsetto
'look dis lovely temateo chile
eddo sixcents a puon
borra, gingy & cassava'
the bass of the blckman
'look nice girl 4 for $1.00
Fresh Hassa'

*Titled by editor

2

But man dis not
dey
dis hea is lon
don bab
ylon
dis dere hea fuh
bring blckman

down, an watch if
na winter ah come
me know dat what
dat got fuh do wit me
when son of sun
touch snow watta got
fuh run
me mean fuh melt dis
with dis african song.

       song.
the colder you get
the hotter I am
angry I am more
than the sun of my
land
so now you see me
laugh you better
start sweat.

TO WHOM THIS POEM MOST CONCERNS

If it is my colour you want
I refuse to give it (no thank you)
you see beneath this colour you
so covet
lies a complicated machine
that motivates these
simplicities

My love - that tension
that releases the fingers
of my hand that is offerred
to you
the eye that looks at you
amazed at the triumph
of the Miracle that makes you
My tongue agast in a million
phrases, astonished that after
all these meetings these times
all thru the innumerable centuries of
a minute's hand-shake
it is my colour you want
I have to offer that love
this hand, this train-crushed
skull
those falling-apart gestures
u laugh so at

This dialect that some
times confuses you amuses you
this too I give - take it
this kingdom of mine, this too
this universe I offer you
my nakedness in incomplete
without this colour
you plead for

I cannot give it for
this is all that is mine
I had forgotten it was there
for this I thank you
having reminded me of its
importance / I refuse
to give it you
take what I offer
take those gifts that
are giveable
My colour is so scarce
supply and demand
you do not need it
for my love you
already have
the sooner I have yours
we can begin that friendship

My voice my words
listen! can tell you tales
that only for this colour
I could not have had
these are mine that I can
give
for if you take my colour
you would lose me

Listen:
in me lies a legion of memory
the long wet journey to strange
lands
the pain of separation
in me lies the memory of
the nailed Jew
pleading for the folly of his fellows
in me lies the screaming
manic
conundrum conundrum conundrum
the madman of dangerous

dreams
he lingers too in the backstep
of my brain
But when I touch the
child's hand a memory
of milk wood time
black as the night is
her breast that I longed
for and sought among the
cotton of her clothes
in me lies the brown Indian
his bow his river
his hands that led me
thru the Marble place
these are me
have me
but my colour I keep
so like the soil
it will soon be
free as the river
hide me as the sea
lighter than the sparrow
sits upon a tree
so light is my caress
the price of my colour is
me
to touch is free
come speak
speak of love
speak of love to
me

LEAP LONG LIGHTLY
LOOPS
LAP THE LAZY LAPLANDER

So it is to meet
oneself in another
time
among crinkled
pages
like a note, in
their sleep

So it is to meet
oneself
like another journeyman
returning
in the closed eye lids
crying babies

Now it is I hear
nothing
but a clock its
heart beat
balancing the rushing
motors
conducting the concert
of birds
I think - yes - alone
I can go - I can stay
I can sleep - I can
stare wide eyed

Summer is in this time
like a calypso

Sleep little now
it is quiet

of human voices and
their echoes

Silence like a geometrical
equation
of sounds
question marks everything
in an all night dawn

What I do I must
what I examine
I do not disturb
my movements like
light
shine the melody of
a nonsense song
until morning
Then the tub

Then the tube

This is a different
cold as if the skin covered
the ice box
I inside like a
ripe apple
being kept for
a ceremony

I think of Plath
and a few other
friends
some not quite
as dead

Death came like
a mist
solid sharp
defined

as the spectrum of
a great plan
of an erroneous
craftman

*A TALE OF TIGER

Scrape Scrape the
wire broom
tiger sweeping the
pavement stone
Dreaming
Dreaming
Now
of going
Home
years like refuse
describe his face
What has TIGER done
so wrong
Whithingham's tale
he took for his
own for fame and
fortune no place
like london twn
Rotten apple cores
cabbages sour &
stink a one
side shoe a bro
ken teeth comb
the gold he found
sifting the gutter
of sand and stone
in this babylon
Scrap scrape the wire broom
tiger sweeping the
pavement stone
Dreaming NOW

*Titled by editor

of home
digging the land
he for 25 years
left alone
to sweep the streets
of this gruel cruel
babylon
his barrow creaking
like insecure floors
rusty hinges on a door
tiger sweeping out
the mews.

his brother with a
mained oilcan
oils his H.P. plan
his metal shine
like a police bootip
reflects as a kick
his dacron groin
then "assassination"
with his hands soaked
in the blood of the can
he scrinches up
tears at the face of
the prime minister of
of England and throws
him in the gutter
scrape scrape the
wire
broom
tiger sweeping the
street clean
Blackwoman with
man chile
suckles her pain
why?
there is no man

she smiles to un
derstan
he has gone leaving
her with the
charity of his
name
scrape scrape the wire broom
tiger sweeping
her plight into the
night where in
defiance it will
ancient ritual
circle beneath the
sodium light
SCRAPE SCRAPE
THE WIRE BROOM
TIGER SWEEPING
in the dawn.

PILOT

I'm sitting with Pilot
in a Nottinghill Gate
cider bar
Pilot's mad black face
studies the racing form
College girls sit &
talk thru paper headlines &
yellow coffee cups

I sit here with Pilot
waiting & wondering
what will happen
I sit here watching
the magic of red buses
the people, the cars, &
colours moving outside in
the electricity of London

An old preacher sips coffee
his prayer book on
a newspaper hiding the
headlines
Pilot's found a Horse
we move out into the
noise becoming part of
the doing

I am moving with Pilot
down a street growing
empty cartons & papers
filled with people smelling
of food

The Juke box digest a sixpence &
belches music

the papers said half of Guiana is
burnt down
I am HERE in Ladbroke Grove
sipping beer & dying
I am here, waiting for Pilot &
watching faces relax &
the sadness I see pains
my eyes,
Guiana is safe in my memory
Politicians are sick jokes
shooting gauldings in the backdam,
This sadness is here
where the bar man plays
Bob Dylan
Not long ago the pavement opened at
a thought and Guiana fell thru
a crack into the vestry of a
printing house
The Classic promises war & peace
for several hours,
Audrey Hepburn stares into
the Frantic side walk with
eyes long tired of war and Peace
I stare into passing eyes
I see only their colours
Pilot plots & points me
to a Pub

I'm in a pub waiting for
Pilot
I think of Guiana
I look for Guiana & find
night workers making the
day
I try to think of Guiana
but the whores eyes are
sad
as one smiles & swears &

grinds her *splendid* emptiness to
a Blue Beat
as she shift her body between the
Spades, a political hunting party
rides thru the Urinal

I take my hand & lead myself out
of this grief
I am in the street of cups
cardboard sales & tourists
I machine gun my sorrow from
behind the green grocers stall
wave to a Guianese in a bus
garage
look in an empty bed for
the sick I go to visit
stare at the bed & realise
all by Myself in one day
I've lost Pilot,
Mislaid a broken legged friend
missed a dinner in Streatham
& found the sorrow of Guiana
in a Pub in Nottinghill Gate....

*HE'S A MOST PECULIAR MAN

He's a most peculiar man
who sings his song to no
one
but to every-one
He's a most peculiar man
with no Honda to go
on the run
a most paculiar man
waking in the morning
he breakfasts
with the sun
He's a most peculiar man
he teaches you something
telling you he cannot stay
He's got to go somewhere to learn
He's a most peculiar man
this one
he ask you for some bathroom space
to brush his teeth and with
a handfull of bush
washes his face
he say he's found that something's
very wrong with what
he'd learnt
so he found a school
to unlearn
this most peculiar man
comes in your office
with a skull cap on
pick his teeth

*Titled by editor

no socks on his feet
he's looking for a job
an Honourable one
looking for a job
like with his degree
can he be your watch man
a most peculiar man
he lives where there's no address
he don't get no mail
that way he says the news
is always fresh
A most peculiar man
you can trust him with your fortune
but he'll steal your mind
and never give you rest
He's a most peculiar man
this one
he ride a smile & talks
about some one being
dispossessed
A most peculiar man
you can give him a meal
& he'll steal your
self assurance
cause he asks you in his company

Please don't smoke a cigarette
it'll make his eyes run
your way is your way
no one knows best
but when you are together
it's happier without
playing with death
cause life he says
can only be lived when the
body has had its rest
He's a most peculiar man
Roy
I think of you now

wondering how one so young
can carry on
smiling and forgiving
where are you
my friend
sitting somewhere
with your hands busy
on some new quest
where are you my friend
comfortable on some corner
or wall
in a home where
you whisper to another
about what you wish for all
is the strength of our spirit
do you see me at all
my friend
will I see you
and remember the way
you screamed with joy
and clasped me to your breast...

He's a most peculiar man... THIS ONE IN YOUR MIDST...

NOW

fr Micheal

It has always
always been that.
that
Singular thought
which no one hears
but all feel
cold like cane
assasinated by
007 machette's
sweat stained steel.
Blood's vision germ-
inating - strengthen-
ing,
creating a FRESH
              NEW
              YEILD

It has always
been THAT
Always THAT
THAT
Singular movement
a cut-eye
a batti-voomps
hands on hips
a hoise of skirt
That fans
the wind into
a raging
mantide.

It has always
always been
that,
that singular
gesture
A hand to
heart
a fist clenched
stabbing air
breaking the
sound barrier
releasing
the cry,
NOW.......
NOW an' dat
sound of
a bass breakin'
pun d-shore of
drums,
Now Now
I standin'
where I belong
D-graves of mi
ancestors a
preciousstone
throne
NOW NOW
I standin' solid
pun firm firm
groun'
cutlass in mi
han chopin' dwn
dem wrongs
NOW NOW

NOW NOW
Standin' Tall
A cedar of
Lebanon
roots strong
fuh
mash dwn
Babylon
overstandin'
d-understandin'
of digital man
NOW NOW
Standin' strong
With
brother suffer
sister
mudda
daughta
fadder
as one war-
head
armed wit
messages frm
we DEAD
NOW NOW
AFRICA
everymothers
chile
a LIVING BOMB
NOW.

IT HAS
ALWAYS,
Always been
That
that
SINGULAR
Thought
that all feel

carrying YOU
On
FRM GENERATIONS
GONE
GENERATIONS TO
COME.
SIGHT
SEEN.

SOMETIMES

Sometimes I does jus
wan fuh lay dwn
quiet, quiet
like grave
wit mi 'oman
head like a
flower growin'
pun mi chest
like a candle
pun all souls
night
neutralizing
d-living
d-dead
d-oppression
an d-wrongs
JUS FUH ONCE.

Sometimes
jus fuh once
I does wan'
siddown fuh
write
wishy-washy
love song
widout ah type
tun bullet an
a machine gun
JUS FUH ONCE.

Sometimes I does
jus fuh once
fuh meditate

pun d-fruitfulness
buried beneath
winter's barren
trees
Widout dat
rush of adrenalin
fuh mystic d-vision
into barbed wired
prison camps.
JUS FUH ONCE
Sometimes I jus
does wan' fuh
hol' mi picknee
innocent han
widout getin'
Slap by d-fact
somewhere dem
busy a plot she
harm,
JUS FUH ONCE.

Sometimes I does
jus wan' fuh
ketch d-rythm
arranged by breeze
fuh trees
an hair
widdout d-crackle
of legislative
papers legalizin'
new methods
fuh dispair.
JUS FUH ONCE
Sometimes I does
jus wan' fuh
hear a shatter
of laughter
an not forced
fuh wonda

how soon before
dat daughter go-
splinter an' splatter
into tears.
JUS FUH ONCE
Sometimes I
does got fuh
consider if
dat .. to ask
jus fuh a second
like dat,
is too much
fuh Africa fuh Ask
Fuh
    jus fuh once.

*I CAN SEE....THE PAST

See the chapel
See the people
See the God
See the steeple
It's falling
        on
The people

Cry not, it is Past

Please I've walked
outside bare
feet
and seen eagles
flying at the
.throats of harmless
women
their wombs preparing
the birth of pigeons
their mouths bleeding
obscenities
and a child swore
at its following
and the cage
flew shut on my
dreaming

It is all past
that waiting
it is all past
that is crying
it has all past

*Titled by editor

prepare now, past
also is the dying
take off not your
hats old women
bow not your heads
old men the
hen stands proud
in the yard the
tamarinds fall
dead sweet and
brown - the shell
at a touch gives
way
I can see the
white verandah
facing the grave
yard
see the hammock
swinging
it is my birthday
the red present wrapped
on the table lies
waiting where she
put it for
me
tomorrow on that
same day I'll
place a gift for her
years whistle by
her slippers forget
the way
years pass by
my nakedness shames
her
years the piling
years
break each gift
forgotten

years oh those
awful growing years
that wished me too
quicking and unprepared
to the hungry breast
of women
years those crying
slipping years
that threw me laughing
into a long valley
covered in their tears
older older I grew
fainter fainter the
cock crew
piling tumbling
from tree top to
bed side
fall malling from
playing to killing
fighting fighting
patriotism to the
parodies of being

U FREAK OUT

20th Century living is a
death BOOM - Listen
the distant moaning
the rasping clang of metal
& wear
the forgotten noise of Guns

Look
Out of a millium of Light
& Silence comes voices
Alien voices with bells
distorted from the past
muddled by the riddle of
years

Listen
the knife the fork the
plate
motors moaning like rain
in a forest night
                    miles away

20th Century living is
a snake pit
films curry aspirins &
astronauts
heard in overcoats & children
voices
seen thru the sleeping
wide eyed
rubber squeaking dolls
all in the raincoat of a
room -

In the damned years
a million pistons ring
the century to a close

There are valleys outside
Hard cold grey stone
lined side by side
edge to edge
wet grey stone splashed
with the white grips of Black tyres

inside is a complicated
combination of tubes
red, grey, black tubes
moving an Army
to keep specimens
working
feel -
busy a million crawling
blood vessels
swam rub grind hold
shake the system of the
mind
further lower lower
they stretch
Wax white - eat it
burn it
it grows on finger nails
it's clear
transparent
it's panic
it melts

Look
those lines criss crossing
the golden threads of eyes
those wire webo crowding
in inner iris of shadows

finger on bone
on plastic
on page
a million piston ring
& the century of man
comes to close

The T.V.
has my head under its
arm
I flap neckless on a
bed   .

A district of
horizontal lives
scream white faced from
the box
Box, black death bands
Brass handles spades dirt
quiet-faced priests with
fertilisers in their hands
mumble sans end sans end
DIRT DIRT DIRT A
FLOOR
the world is a floor of
Dirt to die in

20th Century is celloyde
SELL U LOID
wire light shadow
strings
ink page
mike crow phones
on   off
Red   Green
Light Shadow
a million specks
of
dark dots

white dots
light shadow
hazy shadow
wires tapes lights
strings ink page
  type   type
    ribbon
tape spool
     reel
wind wind
rush rush
scatter scatter
light   shadow
    focus
Light
     metal
         wire
            shadow

words
     light
shines Lines Lines
entire Lines Lines
Lines Lines
       Lines
Lines Lines Lines
          Shine
Line Lines
     Hear see listen
as a million pistons
are ringing the human
century to a
      CLOSE!

*IN THIS AGE OF STRANGLED VISION

In this age of strangled vision
Suped up cars, commercial lies
of promise and £10,000 prizes
for observation of mechanical
durability of household equipment
drenched in psychedelic colours
I walk in the razor sharp night
thinking of words that
could scream across the
wet silent surburban landscape
and burn holes into the
sleep of my brothers
Wake them out of empty
compromise

Words that could erupt
vision of dead bodies
crouching out of the
womb of my young wife
Words to corrupt the
short innocence of my
child's life -
Words that raise the
dead in silhouetted
graveyard
Rotting flesh to wait
at the bus-stop where the
bull rides the bitch
under the sign Request.

*Titled by Editor

I'm straining my ears
thru this Winter's silence
Straining to hear some note
that would free the
constitution of my brain
and release like thunderbolts
my pain -
Lightening erases the black night
with a penetrating dazzling
staggering light
Could my words be like that
Hang from pages, fingers
rotting amputated limbs
to abbreviate my Poem
A window pane of
Amber light screams a baby cry
The trees stand shadows
bare, leafless stumps
on walls as a smaller
night
to this larger one, resting
on the rooftops

A train on high tide
rushes up the beach of silence
My silence echoes back
in my empty self
Staring at a black hill
of derelict cars
it is so I'd like the words
Hugh cumbersome eye sore
difficult to remove
with the dead staring out of
the smashed windows
and twisted frames

My impotence screams
Eerie wooing cats
crouch at the garden gate
their rose bud mouth wide
as in pain
finds an entrance thru
my skin
like a tornado rages in
my black hollow dead brain
then silence
Sharp like a surgeon's
knife incising, festering
rotting skin
Overalls this dead
Marc - lives
In an age of lost vision

Apathetic Political compromise
Vietnam, Ladbroke Grove,
Detroit,
Automatic gear change
Heart transplantations,
Thalidomide

A dead man walks the
empty streets
Evil thoughts try to excite
the brain
A package of blood
free as milk for a
breakfast cereal
Flakes of skin & bone
to pop, crackle & scream
as a pneumatic drill
penetrating a pavement of
stone
Words strong & piercing
the skin as the now

cold drops of Winter's
rain - in my prison of
intellect and flesh
I Scream.

111

GUYANA, MY ALTAR

...on returning my hands should be bloody
for a catalogue of violence erupts
tearing the scab off the scar,
for it is my voice
& the voice of my children
I must win...

*APHORISM No.1

For Penelope & Symon Matthews

Black in a boat
that has no

    name

Sailing on an
ocean window
          pane

looking for fastest
       eater
in a Boat called
rubber

with him is a lady
Doctor

Nurse stays in the
Black house

She
prefers
Land to water

*Titled by Editor

*TO GUYANA, MY ALTAR

to Walter, posthumously

Here in this country that called itself my
mother once, as if black bosoms were not good
enough for my black mouth, here in this country
that fed me cold words monotonous as the ticking
of a clock, as if black words were not rhythmic
enough to sing my heart's song. Guyana on the
maps like some suburban sow her children souse
for a sacrificial supper. Even now that British
hangs on my tongue as a wart removed, but the
scar stings like werre werre pepper. Here in
this strange room of books I find myself bisected,
examined, reconstructed like a myth or extinct
species, maybe if I show myself they may launch
their boat nets, cameras and attempt to preserve
the breed, they already clatter boxes on stone
stairs with some magga brother advertising my
lost stare among his bones, my anger screams
"We are not beggars, advertise your own shame"
the big rancid ladies among the corrupt champagne
and jewels, the china ware and demerara
sugar, the derelict backyards, bitch slush,
your goat bitten damned children, so I fight
for my circumcision from the atrocious whale in
wallowing water. I gaze at these words mine
and not mine, I'm not even free in my dreams,

*Titled by Editor

their planes shatter the landscape of that now
stranger land warped minds home, I kept it close
tight private in the security vault of my skin
eight years on the razor grass I balanced as a
split hair one side cold as dew, the other warm
as EH, EAY, or as white Sartre' in his red coat
close as one against the black gowned Fanon,
Dylan Thomas quiet now silenced by Cesaire explicit
wailing catechism, to a New World the
third world a sprouting jumbi seed in my groin
growing in this iceberg sea. Hate! no it is not
hate but despair that on returning my hands
should be bloody, for a catalogue of violence
erupts tearing the scab off the scar, my silence.
I will not stoop to conquer, for it is
my voice and the voice of my children I must
win, wrest from new missionaries in the reservation;
challenging my morality to rearmament
as if they know that I have sinned.
A further effrontery to my being for only I
can right the wrong, not my wrong. Too long
have they meddled in our affairs with bigotted
pretence that we are children.

      Brothers do you understand
      I who sing the clenched fist
You know the extent of my cowardice
for it is like a grafted tree I grew, neither
one or wholly over to be the other, history's
mangled mutant yet I echo
      After a beneficial internal revolution
      I have come to love this loathsome
      ugliness
And long to freely turn in the trappings

of its incipient black splendour.
    I who carried my typewriter in a wollen
    Sack, now wear it like a holster
    I who leeched the poets prison
    Long for a spade, fork, scythe or hammer
    I who sang the crocus & the fern
    Long to build Rorima empire
    I who sought to be High Priest
    Sacrifice now myself
    To Guyana my altar
    Or my blood in some
    Arid alien land
    Must turn to water
    Enough - Marc
    What do you
    Bring with this offer
    The lessons of poverty
    Thirst & hunger
    Poverty my warm
    Blessed blood brother
    Efficient teacher & keeper.

THE SOUND OF SILENCE

There is a terrible
Silence banging
Thru this land
a silence dat loading
gun
Clanging Prison door
A silence louder
than the screams of
the Tortured
Silence following
like a carnival
an passin' you wit -
a fan
    fare
Silence a Ol'Higue
sucking the blood
of Promise frm
childrens lives
rumbling through
this land
A stone crushing
silence
leaving anti-men
swearing bubbles
in the neck of Rum
Bottles
A silence a salt
sucking silence
if you look good
you can see it
watch it Dea
insanely staring
at imperial skies

See it dea
flashing it knife
swing it cutlass
see it spinning it
web of violence
Hear it hear it
listen good
listen
The water tasting
of gaul
an ah see D.River
it clot   wit
blood
cover up yo head
is not rain Dis
is pus
Listen listen to
articulate silence
They put electric
microphones
in me head
shouting digits
to a micro-clock
Listen listen
to dat silence
OH - Mi Mamma - O
O - Mi Mamm - O
Dem tek me sista
an infect she
wit poison
An wuk
she
Behin the latrin
Tief she wit
advertisment
A wuk she

in a Mer-
cedez
Benz
When dem juk she
an juk she
O me mammo
O mi mammo
No body na see
No body na hear
an everybody bin
Dere
Wit me sissi & me
O - me Mammo - O
O - Me Mamma - O
Me telling you
Dis silence so
loud - me sure
you Kyan even
Hear yr self
Breathe.
Is Klean
X
invent
sneeze.

SUSU

SHE
SAY THAT
HE
SAY THAT
'it didn't go SO,
but so, when ting
see ting, yo knw
Ting does see
RED, So he Ting
pull out he ting
to put a tining
pun ting. But Ting
see D-ting an' knw
say was a real real
ting,
So ting run an'
hide bottom a ting
AND is right dere
dat watumacallit
get d-ting 'rong

cause wasn' dat
tingamagig fall
dwn, but d-ting next
to dat ting.'
well I don't get
no more bout
d-ting, cause
bus reach Brixton
an I had fuh do
A TING.

EYE - PASS

When it happen
it
does get ya
go rite thru
yo

get ya right hea
in the pit

it does get ya

get ya
pass the testimonals
of terror

all the
Congos
the
Sowetos
the
Sudans
the cowering
crouching
Caribbean
get ya
get ya
Pass all dat
all the Cudjoes
the Cuffys
the
Rodneys
It does
get ya

rite hea
rite hea
pass the clones
of California
pass Littlewoods
and
they one point eight
millions
pass the spring
sales spilling
on the week's
street
ahh say it
does get ya
pass the affairs
of passion
pass the elegant
silver plates of
grace pass
the smiling light
in the gloom
pass the missionary's
success
the heavenly rendezvous
snuggling in snuggledowns
pass
the nostalgic past

get ya
get ya

like a knock
on yr funny bone

ah say! When it
happen it
does get ya

get ya BAD
badder dan bad
bad for days

When! When!
ya know
dem clappin'
to the mournin'
marching blck
family feet
carting dem
contribution to
bring the un-
employmant figures
down
      down
burying a loved
son
if !!!
it does get
ya!!!
get ya so
ya
boil and burn
get ya so
ya want to
grab gun
obeah all
an start
something
and let it out
once and for all
win, lose or
draw
let it rass
done
jus fuckin' done!

and pun top
all dat
the
light-bill
come.

REALARRO

I love the
friday night
smell of
mammie baking
bread - creeping
up to me in
bed
& tho I fall
asleep before I
even get a bite
I know for sure
when
morning come
the kitchen table
will be laden
with bread
fresh & warm.
salt bread
sweet bread, crisp
& brown &
best of all
coconut buns
make me
love the friday
night smell of
mammie baking bread
putting me to bed
to sleep
dreaming

AH DADDY DIS

Yes! Me daddy is story
fire come fuh
ELIJAH
was hurricane
come fuh me daddy
an' the win' blow
Mountain & Morne
like conch shell
an the watta hoise
up itself
an' tek way the
lan'
Yes. Me daddy
ride 'ahm
profane temple
gutted by wind
& watta
100,000's dollars
brick wood & mortar
a matchstick roun'
the mountain neck
Dominica feel Passova
an the militant
cower &
10 year tiefing plans
debris & straw
& cleanzin
a humblin for
stiff neck Politicians
yes
when it pass it
did don' pick up
me daddy

Yes he bin a
ride 'ahm
An frm Calcuni
to Potatro
the tribes see
Kanima
An dem hear he
voice lik a echo
an when he gone
the villages sweep
clean of the proud
triva
the land fresh & new
like it born again
yes
Me daddy bad for days
when he talk
he make yo' laugh
yr laughter
&
shed yo tears
he chop down
silk cotton tree
Yes me daddy
wha me X me!
ketch lightening in
he han'
wit a thunder bolt
in the palm
Yes
ME daddy eat
passion fruit
an drink wine
in 1949
Banish ole 'Higue
chase masacurra-

man
when he touch
moongazer hair
stan pun
end -
When coolie jumbie
ask ME DADDY
'Ever see Teet like
dese?', 'Yes'
ME DADDY tell he
'Better shut yo
mout for me
make yo swallow
ahm'
Jumbie run -
Too much time
ME DADDY refuse
O.B.E.
too much time
he chase
whiteman - he
jes lay in
hammock an
Halla pam ahm
yes
Fire come for
ELIJAH
an the cloak
fall fuh ELISHA
ME daddy smile
before he go long
an gie the gown
to we Queen
ME MAMMIE
yes
in the year Jah

1979
ME daddy get
fetch by
Hurricane - an
passova the
Caribbean -
if yo feel ah
lie -
check yr file -
pepper blow in yo
eye -

FOLKSONG

for Harry Crossman

I am the sorcerer
Me navel string
Bury Bottom
a Sankoka Knee.
Me daddi walking stick
is a coconut tree -
He spitoon D. Sea

Chorus
I/We are sorcerers
Ol' Grady fire
Baptize me
I am the answer
to every Ma-Riddle-ma
Ree.

Chorus
I/We are sorcerer
Ti Jean
is me brother
Sakanbola
Me sponsor

Rick Chic Chic
Conga tey
yo' see fowl
omma
Tell she i dea
Hea

Chorus
Watch man fun
sun
Moon companion
I am - that I am a league of nations

'...*wld you help to sing/these songs of freedom/all I ever heard...*'
(hon Br B Marley)

REDEMPTION SONG

for Kamal & Maya

A middle ah night
metal arrested
by d-fire in d-
street light
Apples oranges
issuing shadows
cross ah floor
picking up d-vibes
coming alive in
1905,
walter footprints
deep in the dust.

    . 1
No domino nah
chop
No Ca'd nah
flash
pun ah table top
No Cheefa man
Nah
'nack ah-mi door
No dice nah roll
cross ah floor.
AND
Down by ah water-
front

No ship nah load
Inna factory no
cane Nah grine.
NAH!
LONG WALK, WHA
STA'T FUH WA'K
GRASS
Frighten fuh dem
neck when
a man walk
pimpla spot 'im
stride, dem
genuflect,
Befo 'im footbottom
glass bottle run
inna d-grass fuh
hide.
watch 'im
mark he good
years ah sufferin'
cutlass sharp
he face
every bad john
clear out ah man
walkin'space,
'im beckon nobody
fuh say
'FALLA ME'
He word is d-deed,
wha mek a long
suckteet
blanket ah lan'
        AND
everybody dat is
somebody
trn shadow behin'

ah man,
all cane dun cut
all duttie dun dig
all factory close
down
Is 1905 an December
jus'get born
What D-finga' cyan
write
d-foot dea fuh
shout it out,
every body dat is
any body marchin'
wit dem voice
    And
dea right dea
behin' ah-man
time come
fire fire
bun me
han', mighty
Blck Right
gainst White
Capital Wrong

the pendulum of time
makes circles of our
lives..
d-bakra gone, yet
d-bull dog feasts
& the eagle's remains
is wha
d-carrion crow
eats.

Long Walk, Hear!
walk yo talk,
make dem hear

'Whea Pimpla juk
yo foot, same
place fuh tek it
OUT.
Dubbin' d-vibes
is 1905

Nah Dec 1st
    AND
gun Nah sta't
Pop

an' a bullet of dat
day, did ricochet
to fin' it way
into 1980
to june 23rd
Walter's life
interred
it is the same
bullet that
father drake knew
as a knife
the selfsame bullet
that found it's way
between clover &
spice to claim
Maurice's & Martin's
life. Bullet
born of musket ball
& powder
shattered seasons
Africa, India, China
To feed the greed of
conglomorate vampire empires.

The pendulum of time makes
circles of our lives,

Rio de historias
tan amorgo de la agonicas
  Rio de historias
  incapaz de memorias
  confunde con las rocas
  el ojo del agua mira la verdad
  es la verdad del agua mira
  es verdad agua
    es este
    es este - vive
    vive, vive ya

     2
  va venir
  el dia
  una luz reciente
  aspecto de fuego
  salpicaduras de una llama
  que se ailmenta con la llama
  alcazar al futuro
  es este
  es este
  vive vive vive
  vive pueblo vive
  por
  Biko
  Ghandi
  Shabazz
  Che
  Lumumba
  all the victims
  of that, which
  was born of
  ball & powder
  spawning bombs
  frm the artic

thru the tropics
of cancer.
Dubbed in a
1905 refrain

NAH
dec 1st, Nah
nah bobby chapman
wah get shot
a yng man life
dat bullet stop.
Is 1905 again,
NAH
After   all
dat   strain
              all
dat   pain
              all
dat   shit
              all
dat   rain
              all
              all
dem babies
              all
buried in
cardboard
box
all all all
all man nah
down dem muscle
nah all wuk stop
an ova d-town
ah sky nah open
an' let loose
an centepede rain.

      when sidedam bus
      flood is a mus'
      an is bus it bus
No cane nah cut
No duttie nah dig
Dec 1st
overflow an' wash
when yuh Kata
weigh dwn wid
     sorrow
an' yuh waist ban'
rotten wid misery
nuttin but win'
fuh fill manbelly
yuh GOT fuh get
red of d-gripes inna
yuh brain
an vision nah mus'
mek mission
an the voice of ancestors
like blood pun stone
let loose de groans
frm the holds of
forgotten ships
fuh reah Rorima's tip
fuh greet mazaruni's
precious river bed
to d-drains in
Nigger yard
Bound yard
yard wid no
name
measured the years
in savage days
bloody hours, toll
the flesh, with out

and with in,
wid she han pun
she hip
Dorothy Rice, pickup
d-stick
bear witness
she swell wid pride
to she rightful size
She NAH mek fun
D-eyepass done
No dish nah wash
No clothes nah i-ron
No sheet nah heng out
fuh air
No floor nah sweep
No dust nah dus'
No step nah scrub
No brass nah polish
No silver nah shine
No shoe nah clean
No pot nah cook

No baby cart nah
                push
D-eye pass done
she pelt way d-cap
tear off ah apron
her labour, the
sweetness in dem
life
she got fuh suck
d-salt of dem
vice,
cool as watta in-
na drought
1905

dorthy rice
voice
name her rightful
price
Come shantyman
kaiso storyteller
dub musician
invoke the nation
wit songs of we
glorious STRONG.

So stood the people
firm as light
between the shadow
of war ships that
came
bold bees between
bayonets as thorns
in the garden cities
of wrongs.
Righteous as breath
the heroes stand
side by side
with heroines strong
before the carrion
of gain.

Sing loud their names
pour libations
to baptize we young.
Teach the wisdom of
dem seeing
the sightin'
reasoning in dis
springtide of sufferin'

Sing the loud nightlong
a battle chant
pluck the rotten
purple fruit
wrinkled dry
crapo skin it
strangles breath &
blood
of the promised yng

Pluck it
uproot, turn the
earth & prepare
for a new harvest
a fertile dawn.
Under a shameface sun
in a trembling afternoon
here on a kentish
foreshore
the breeze start a bawl
frm a guyana sea wall
an a hearin' all, all
guyana's maga belly
scream of village
women
O mi momma O
O mi momma O
Hungry belly cyan
mek babywatta
grave open like
koka
O mi momma O
O mi momma O
Dis time nah long time
Dis time nah befoe time
dis time a-woserer time

Worserer dan anytime
man cyan remember
Plantatian gone
Yet manager
    overseer
    driver
is dem wha tekova
O mi momma O
O mi momma O
dem get ahm fuh nuttin'
dem ah eat ahm fuh glutten
an' leff awee fuh fare
pun salt watta
O mi momma O
O mi momma O
trobi, trobi
Sani moro guyana
Sani moro guyana
               Ca vrai
               Ca vrai
C'est la meme moen perdi
      gangan moen
C'est la meme moen perdi
      ganpa moen
moen ca debat pour la vie
Sani moro
Sani moro
Trobi
Trobi
               Ca vrai
Ca dia
               Ca vrai
Hay cadaveres   Ca vrai

CHANT NOW

For a
re-awakening
Give ancient voices
release - from
the swamps of for-
get
full
ness.
From Corriverton
to the Amazon
Let the archeries
of energy
run as rivers
frm High land
to Low land.

Seawall -
that
On This Stranger's wall
this mudhead beach
Guyana finds Guyana
on a Kent foreshore
Sees Brown river
playin' las lick wit
a Brown sea. An de shore jetty
where passion, Death,
fertility hook together
wit' one concrete Juwat
ah plough history soil

Come darkness dying'
Loose out D-string'

Let D-bull dem
sing
A ressurection song
Easter Monday
    Morning

        Come lea we go pun
        D-seawall - lille bit
        fuh   lille bit
        Lille   bit
        feel up
        Lille   bit
        Rub up
        Lille bit   bit
        Jukin' man Jetty
        Inna Madame Sea
        Lille   bit
        one one juk-juk
        mek baby
        mek saga boy turn
                daddy
        mek sweet gal turn
                mammie
        pun one family size Chubbie
        Brace up pon a wall
        Listenin' to a baby
                bawl
        echo inna sea
                Come Come
        lea we go
        Pun d-sea wall
        Sunday bes
        Pretty dress
        Parade an Pose
        basadi wit tiepi
        forceripe love story.

                    Come Come
lea we go pun
D-seawall
Bus D-bottle
Sing D-song
pitch we XM melody
gainst D-sea
watchin the overboards
wit - dem short-time
Cast-net ketchin'
Respectable
Bigfish
No rent fuh pay
Seawall like backseat
always free.
Come lea we go
pun D-seawall
talk ole time story
debat questions
political with
plantation philosophy
watch Dem picknee
like crab march
dance an play
duck an drake in
d-sea

Come lea we go
pun-d-seawall
Cut d-baby hair
tek it - mek sacrifice
to mumma sea
gather fuh make puja
puja
throw the flowers
garland d-sea

Come - Baptize
Duck the New Born
Come Read the word
Sister
fire nex time roun'
Come buil the
pyre
pour D-gee
Light D-fire
Scatter D-ashes
inna D-sea

Come Come
Lea we go
pun D-seawall
See if Fairmaid
Leff she comb
fuh we.

DO FAIRMAID...

How you can
Bean Hear
maga
belly's shrill
siren screams of
Village women's
call

Omi mumma O
Omi mumma O
Sani moro Guyana
hard guava season
reach awee, lobi, lobi
yo na see
wite mout rampant
pun awee
Babra gone, but
cutanload
like am neva done
pashuma - malnutrition
kalhari - deep iron pan
pashuma a graze
Suckin' dry de lan'
pun Bannas
pun Binni
Owi Megoy
Owi Megoy
fair maid
Na cut yo-eye
pun awee
fairmaid na-
tell me say
Yo Na hear

Yo Na see
Jun Juh
a cova awee
Release
D Voice of
Mazaruni
    history
frm Konashen
to Mabaruma
frm Karikan
to Courantyne
coloured anato
cotton an' cofee
to HRM Sugar
frm passage
to pastures
wreathing
Ancestors
Wake dem
Wake dem
Wipe d-boo boo
from dem eye
d-wax out
dem ear
Mex dem see
Mex dem wit-
ness - gie back we
Burden of freedom
Bruk de tengeleh - crab pinchers
pimpla thorn
haul out d-
pimpla
an husk out
d-stain ah-
corruption
from awee

O mi momma O
O mi momma O
Wa na quendeh
Sa quendela
O mi momma O
Mex dis TININ BEN
Mex dis
Story End.
Do fairmaid do
A - do -